FIVE FIELDS

Also by Gillian Clarke from Carcanet

The King of Britain's Daughter
Selected Poems
Collected Poems

For my mother, Gwendolen Ceinwen Evans (1912-1997)

Five fields, five oceans,
seven continents.
So little.

Acknowledgements

Acknowledgements are due to the following publications where some of these poems, or versions of them, first appeared: *Klaonica, Poems for Bosnia*, Bloodaxe; *Poetry Wales, Picture Poems*, edited by Michael and Peter Benton, Hodder & Stoughton; the organ recital programme 1997-1998, the Bridgewater Hall, Manchester; *Alchemica*, Oriel Mostyn; *The Third Day*, edited by Kathy Miles, Gomer Press; *Christmas in Wales*, edited by Dewi Roberts, Seren Press. 'Green Man' is included in *Thirteen Ways of Looking at Tony Conran*, edited by Nigel Jenkins for the Welsh Union of Writers. 'The City' and 'Concerto' were commissioned by the Bridgewater Hall, Manchester and first broadcast on Radio 3 in 1997. 'Ark' was commissioned by Poetry International, Rotterdam, 1996. 'Valley', 'Into the Mountain', 'Layers of Melancholy', and versions of 'The Paddle-Steamers' and 'Light' were commissioned by Oriel Mostyn, Llandudno for an exhibition of sculpture. My version of 'Passus xi' from *A Vision of Piers Plowman* by William Langland was commissioned by the Royal Festival Hall, London, for Poetry International.

Special thanks are due to the Arts Council of Wales for a bursary which helped me to write some of these poems, and to the Bridgewater Hall, Manchester, for commissioning 'The City' and 'Concerto' during my residency in May, 1997.

Contents

The Field-Mouse

Summer, and the long grass is a snare drum,
The air hums with jets.
Down at the end of the meadow,
far from the radio's terrible news,
we cut the hay. All afternoon
its wave breaks before the tractor blade.
Over the hedge our neighbour travels his field
in a cloud of lime, drifting our land
with a chance gift of sweetness.

The child comes running through the killed flowers,
his hands a nest of quivering mouse,
its black eyes two sparks burning.
We know it'll die, and ought to finish it off.
It curls in agony big as itself
and the star goes out in its eye.
Summer in Europe, the fields hurt,
and the children kneel in long grass
staring at what we have crushed.

Before day's done the field lies bleeding,
the dusk garden inhabited by the saved, voles,
frogs, a nest of mice. The wrong that woke
from a rumour of pain won't heal,
and we can't face the newspapers.
All night I dream the children dance in grass,
their bones brittle as mouse-ribs, the air
stammering with gunfire, my neighbour turned
stranger, wounding my land with stones.

Barn

1

Where the wheelbarrow slumps, a lake of rust in its lap,
where rolls of chicken wire loll, caging
a wilderness of nettle and yellowing grass,
where leftover timber rots into cities of woodlice,
you see a barn. Dumpy level, tape, clipboard,
and I'm frozen to the bone. One dawn I'll be glad of it,
the graphite lines raised to a grid of steel
on the icy sky, roof on, walls firm, and me
in some strawy corner with the black-faced ewe,
the smell of hay, of birth, their private cries
and the first birds singing.

2

In a field of *fescue, timothy* and *Yorkshire fog*,
two swallows skim the pond for flies,
rehearsing reflections for the long haul south.
And you up there where the new barn rises,
your hair bleached with summer,
climbing the spaces of your own geometry,
already see light fall through a window
on orderliness: workbench, tools oiled and graded,
the timber stacked in aromatic piles.

You pull me into the sky to see the sea,
the purple mountains of the north. You say,
'We'll have a telescope, a barn owl box'.
I see us grow old under the poetry of stars,
listening for snowfall of owl. You steady me
on the ladder's trembling summit, all sky about us,
earth askew and spinning, the lake upside down,
swallows dreaming Africa in this first September chill.

Shepherds

Night of the black moon.
Above the house, Venus
bright as a lamp.
The field glitters in the flashlight
with the thirty stars of their eyes.

Somewhere the croak of a bird
and far off, chained
in the yard of a nameless farm
a dog barks. Downwind
the smoke of our dying fire.

In the unsteady light of the torch
you shoulder the bale, break it,
ram the racks with the needling sweetness
of nettle-scents, herbs, the trapped breath
of thirteen kinds of summer grasses.

The ewes are pushy,
Blackface first to the bucket,
then the one who hooves our shoulders
to hurry the mumble
of our iron hands.

You call from the dark –
first lambs steaming in lamplight.
We carry them in, one each, hot and yolky
with their strange scent of the sea,
the ewe in a panic at our heels.

Above us in the Square of Pegasus
a satellite wavers
like a torch in a field.

Ark

'Keeping the seed alive upon the face of all the earth once the fountains of the deep and the windows of the sky are stopped.'

Genesis

1

Winter of rain, the rivers of Europe too big for themselves,
and the oceans rising. The sea's at the door. It curls into the cellar,
climbs the stairs, laps the threshold of cities.
Coastal towns go under. A church falls to the waves.
Only the watchman awake to cry 'flood' in the drunken palace
as the wall is breached and the sea takes Cantre'r Gwaelod.
Only a boy with his thumb in the dyke as the low countries drown.

2

From Oxfam, an ark of gopher wood,
each beast so crude I can't name it for sure:
elephant, tiger, zebra, two maned lions, no lioness,
white creatures tall as camels or giraffes.
Could they be sheep?

3

Rain falls through February, March.
'Of every clean beast thou shall take to thee by sevens.'
Beulah Speckle-faced, and three black faced ewes.
The flock puddles the field to mud.
We wake nightly in the early hours, dress for the rain,
to count their faces in the flashlight, their glittering eyes.

A sudden day of light and the March wind's home
like a hare running. The flock is moonlit cloud,
their breath starlight. One ewe stands alone
turning and turning, pawing the ground.
The horizons in the gold-green of her eyes
know the midwife in me before I do.

You hold her shoulders and talk tenderly.
The scalding cave's familiar as soapy washing,
in my hand a sodden head, the slippery pebbles
of hooves. Out of the bone ark adrift
on its flood I bring the lamb. Its skull
is the moon on my palm,

the four of us murmuring, earthed again,
getting our bearings.

Flesh

1

On a frozen morning in November
the wethers walk to their death.
Not a sound but their muffled foot-notes
on the stony road. No hurry or fuss.
In the barn tonight they'll be quiet
as the five fields of their lives
since the March day they were born.

Tomorrow one after another
stone still on the hard earth
they'll stand for the gun.
His thumb on the dead-bolt.
Silence will flood the chancels.
In the stunned air something will give,
will forget what it was to be born.

The man will work, wordless and calm,
till the job's done. Each fleece folded,
blood and the smell of slaughter
sluiced from the shed after every lamb.
Something will stop, breath held
in a yard awash with water.

2

In Memoriam

Bitter cold. Three hundred
remember a friend, glad of the living
in the frozen ribcage of the church.

The hymns know what death is:
darkness in the skull of the lamb
at the flick of a thumb,

in the widow's breast
a slow explosion
in the muffled heart,

in our throats, ice,
her weeping stars,
the glacier in the bone.

2

On its hook in the barn
the carcase is clean,
a licked bone from the sea.

He hands me two suet-caskets.
When I break them open,
with the whisper of tearing,

and hold in my hands the cold
soft weight of the kidneys
before slipping them from their silk,

they'll be the wet stones
of a lamb's hooves,
the slippery ball of its head

in the birth-flood,
they will be the heart
of the new-born beating,

imagining the dead
in their cold places,
flesh in its fire and ice.

Neighbour

The barn floor's cleared for the month of tractor,
mower, timber-pile, to make way for stalls,
sweet oils of sawn timber and tools displaced
by breaths of hay, wet fleece and lanolin.

He backs the pick-up in between the doors,
vaults the hurdles like a boy, his overalls
fresh from unfolding. He lifts a lamb from the straw,
slipping the leaves of its ears between his fingers,
takes a crease of woolly skin too big for it,
unloads the hypodermic into the fold.

With the lamb in his arms, he talks of politics,
and stars, the trip I'm making to Arabia,
the article he'll write for the *papur bro*
on how the Sheikha and her women live,
and how the oil has altered all their lives,
the price of lamb, the cruel practices
of the meat industry, if I'll see the same stars
over the desert, how it was better for lambs
in the old days, how we'll wreck the earth with greed.

He hugs the lamb, rubs his cheek against it,
draws its leafy ear between his fingers.
'A fine ram lamb,' he says, and sets it again
beside its mother stamping in the straw.

A Difficult Birth, Easter 1998

An old ewe that somehow till this year
had given the ram the slip. We thought her barren.
Good Friday, and the Irish peace deal close,
and tonight she's serious, restless and hoofing the straw.
We put off the quiet supper and bottle of wine
we'd planned, to celebrate if the news is good.

Her waters broke an hour ago and she's sipped
her own lost salty ocean from the ground.
While they slog it out in Belfast, eight decades
since Easter 1916, exhausted, tamed by pain,
she licks my fingers with a burning tongue,
lies down again. Two hooves and a muzzle.

But the lamb won't come. You phone for help
and step into the lane to watch for car lights.
This is when the whitecoats come to the women,
well-meaning, knowing best, with their needles and forceps.
So I ease my fingers in, take the slippery head
in my right hand, two hooves in my left.

We strain together, harder than we dared.
I feel a creak in the limbs and pull till he comes
in a syrupy flood. She drinks him, famished, and you find us
peaceful, at a cradling that might have been a death.
Then the second lamb slips through her opened door,
the stone rolled away.

A Very Cold Lamb

With a book to finish and umpteen things to do,
here I am kneeling in straw, with a young ewe
fussing and mothering about me, drying the lambs
she slithered from her hot womb into the stream
where we found them, took them for frozen or drowned.
Working together, my hair-drier and her breath,
we warm two shivering lambs from the brink of death.
One is so cold it can't open its mouth to cry
for shaking, shaking hungry death by the throat,
that fox with a taste for soft tissue, that bird of doom
after each intricate beautiful brain, each eye.
We work for an hour, the drier humming, the ewe
licking their syrups with her passionate tongue,
calling the blood to their limbs, liver, lungs,
each womb as small as a nut. The two lambs strive.
They're warming to the idea of staying alive.

Rain

A light across the garden through the rain
that silks itself all day into the earth,
through porous shale into the aquifers,
deeper and deeper finding its way to bedrock.

A light through the smoke of rain from the barn
where he strokes curls of wood through the mouth of the plane,
shaving the sap-rings where the tree once drank
its prodigious sips of old deep water.

We'll both think, 'who are you?', when he comes in
through the falling rain and we stand in the light of a room
seeing each other strange again after nothing
but seas breaking between the continents.

His hands will be sappy with sycamore, oak or pine,
whatever he's been easing through oiled steel,
familiar as rain, the tools, and pages. The house
will reclaim us, offering firelight, music, a glass of wine,

after the rain and the oceans between us, grace,
landfall, the communion of a gaze.

Architect

When he sets his board in the long grass of Perigord
in the ellipse he mowed under the *prunus niger*,
as to the one star of a house on the mountain,
all earth's lines come running to him:

Gossamers, corn-drills, bean-rows, Roman roads and passes,
poplars lined-up all ways over deep grasses,
massive limestone in the mason's yard,
rusting steel girders, sawn timber, scented wood,

a tractor mumbling down hill, deliberate,
slow and measured, trying to get things straight
all the hay-making afternoon, overhead
the swallows' tangled airy latitudes.

All day, a 3H pencil on its compass turning
and weighed with its own shadow, the red tree burning.

The Honey Man

The tin trunk rusts in a red pool
with its cargo of old frames,
crumbling honeycomb dark with pollens
and a dried glisten of wings
from dead summers.

By the gate, six feet from the car,
the abandoned hive the wild swarm
took over last year, that we meant
to move in winter as they slept
before the March sun woke them.

From the car we watch behind glass.
He comes through the dusk
in his space suit and veil,
charming the bees with smoke
from the swung censer.

He lifts off the roof
and is jewelled with bees.
The air strums with a million stings
as they settle on the glass eye to eye
with the children.

At moonrise, before bed, they take turn
to press their ears against the hive,
to breathe in the honey and hear
a million cooling wings beat
like a city in a box.

Phoning Home

She sounds so small and frail I can't believe it.
In the real time her hair was red
and I was small and she taught me all I knew.
We say goodbye. I'll phone again. Soon.
Take care. Don't fall. Sit on the balcony in the sun.
Take a walk on the green. Mind you eat properly.

And in the post that photograph of her
lent to the television company.
It's sixty years ago and harvest time.
She leans in muslin against barley stooks
singing with ripe seed and I'm not born,
and he, long ago, the tranced photographer.

Why must it happen last, old age,
come to steal everything,
leaving us warned of what there is to lose,
relishing this, this sunlit yellow moment
of grief in the post,
grief on the telephone?

Glass

AT THE GLASS FACTORY

The recipe is lead, sand, fire,
dangerous treacles spun for the tourists.
Before our eyes a goblet forms
in the sun-shaft of particles burning
with light off the Lagoon.
It stills to ice, becomes
contained stillness,
a canal of smoky water,
cupful of light ready
to be burnished with a clean white cloth.

HER TABLE

She fussed between kitchen and dining room
giving us all things to carry and do.
I see her two hands polishing a wine glass
until it gleams, immaculate.
She lifts it to the light and sets it down
on starched damask on the Christmas table.

On an ordinary Sunday it would be
a cut-glass jug of water, four tumblers.
As if these things could hold us, as if
they could make us flawless and ring true.

THE HABIT OF LIGHT

In the early evening, she liked to switch on the lamps
in corners, on low tables, to show off her brass,
her polished furniture, her silver and glass.
At dawn she'd draw all the curtains back for a glimpse
of the cloud-lit sea. Her oak floors flickered
in an opulence of beeswax and light.
In the kitchen, saucepans danced their lids, the kettle purred
on the Aga, supper on its breath and the buttery melt
of a pie, and beyond the swimming glass of old windows,
in the deep perspective of the garden, a blackbird singing,
she'd come through the bean rows in tottering shoes,
her pinny full of strawberries, a lettuce, bringing
the palest potatoes in a colander, her red hair bright
with her habit of colour, her habit of light.

SHOPPING

Brought up with make do and mend, she wanted nice things.
Saturday shopping and afternoon tea at *The Angel*,
after haberdashery and household linen she'd move
in a trance through departments of china and glass
in the big city stores. As she moved, light sang
on the rims of tea-cups and glasses.
The shimmer stayed with her, reflecting her face
when she unpacked the parcels on the kitchen table
that stood on worn linoleum they couldn't afford to replace.

UNDER THE STAIRS

Then, I think it was winter,
an air-raid siren,
the far thump where the bomb fell
and the ramparts gave.

That piece of shrapnel we held
and showed to neighbours,
proud to be hit, to be alive.
I took it to school in a matchbox
like a tame meteorite.

How could it be so cold and small
after melting glass,
after biting a hole in the dining room window,
after burning a hole in the rust carpet,
after trying to get me under the stairs?

MIGRAINE

Here it comes again: vision bevel-edged
with rainbows, stuff dissolving even as I look
to liquid light, the firm world swimming
just beyond the rim of things.

There's a remedy today: the *migraleve*
they gave me from her medicine cupboard,
I being the daughter who'd inherited this,
and her skin, and the early grey in our hair.

It's the last thing I should be doing,
squinting at a screen at the still centre,
getting the words down before the onset
of vertigo and steel drums.

Then all I'll want is the green curtains drawn
in her room in the afternoon, sun-arrows splintering
her dressing table to a clutter of brushes and combs,
dustings of powder, its lipsticks and eau de cologne.

And her duck-down pillows and old-rose eiderdown,
her hand weightless and cool on my brow,
changing the scalding flannel for the cold one.
'A sick headache', they called it, when I was an infant.

She taught me to lie so still, the pain wouldn't find me.
If I drifted to sleep, she would creep away,
lifting her cool hand
too lightly to wake me.

THE CROQUET SET

A box of varnished wood,
frayed rope handles at each end.
Every year on the first day of summer
he'd ease the creak from the hinges
with a trace of green, iridescent oil.

Eight worn mallets, their shafts warped,
blue, yellow, purple. Mine was the red one.
The brown one nobody wanted. Hoops, posts,
eight wooden balls, all colour
knocked out of them, and the rules lost.

No rush. No slapdash setting out.
She stepped into the garden with a tinkling tray
as he mowed the lawn to stripes, unruled his tape
over the grass. The knock of wood on wood,
our shadows so long we were taller than trees.

The man takes cash, knocks fifteen pounds off.
This one's from a French château,
but under the lid it's all mine now
and I take back from the dark one hour so bright
there seemed an even chance of getting it right.

QUINCE

I planted a quince for her, completing the ellipse
of fruiting trees – plum, apple, an apricot
grown from a stone – for its colour and grace.
But six weeks after her death, it's not the bitterness
of quince that has me by the throat again,
but the *acer* tossing its red hair
under the running skies of May,
the tree whose leaves she untangled
with hands that untangled my hair.

CUT GLASS

'She wanted you to have them,' he said.
'She knew you'd look after them.'
We polish them, her favourite cut glass,
making diamonds and rainbows.
She loved sparkle, parties, a ball-gown
with rhinestones, a touch of diamanté.
She knew she was luminous
looking up from her sherry glass.
Even I felt my heart leap then.

ELEGY

'Place but a kiss within the cup,'
my father used to sing.
We drink from her glasses,
and I know you're thinking as we sip
that she touched them with her hands and lips.

Grief is diamond hard. It engraves the story on glass,
leaves nothing out. Sunlight swims on this page,
this table, in the tumbler of water like a shoal
of moving shallows, not quite shadows, or smoke,
as the glass hardens and clears.

We fill our goblets with water,
cold pure risings from deep
beneath our garden.
Each glassful is archaeology,
brimmed seepings
that have taken life-times to collect.

Into her crystal sherry glasses
pour us a *Fino*. Then a good wine
into fine Venetian crystal.
With this libation I remember her,
hold it to the light,
touch your glass with mine
on a pure note.

Amber

Coveted week after week on the market stall,
coiled, nonchalant, arrayed under the lid
of locked glass, they grew familiar.
She'd finger them, drop them over her head,
try them for size, spoilt for choice –
red-amber, yellow, cut Russian ruby,
or those sad rosaries, widow's beads of Whitby jet.
In each bead surfaced the cloudy face of a woman.

Warmed by the sunlight on dressing tables,
or against a woman's skin, then laid safe
in a drawer each night between the silk leaves
of her underwear. Never cold, as if
each bead were an unquenchable flame
that burned a million years like a sanctuary lamp
beneath the ice, each drip of sticky gold
hardening to honeyed stone.

As if nothing that has ever contained heat
can be cold again, mirrors never empty
and our rooms, furniture, hoarded amulets,
could reassemble themselves into a life
and still pass hand to hand from underneath
the permafrost, ice woman to living daughter.

The White Ship

On the kitchen table he made me a ship –
war on the wave-lengths,
Children's Hour, tea,
and the roads locked in snow.

The News was dark with sinkings,
shadows in the sea, talk of U-boats,
sinister submarine things
that could tow you down.

What signal calls it back now?
The hull in his hands,
bone-webbed, fingerprinted
among slivers of wood and glue.

We came home from the beach,
with a wreckage of leavings –
oiled ropes, driftwood,
a crate of oranges.

So he built my boat
from a baulk of ship's timber
thrown up in a storm
from the war-wounded sea.

He worked all that winter,
set a radio in the engine-room,
then painted her white
as the ship on every horizon.

One Sunday in spring
we launched her on the lake.
'*The Queen Mary*,' he said
as she slipped his hands.

She set off for perilous waters
in a scatter of swans and marvelling boys,
dancing to port and starboard,
till her course set westwards

at the star of my will. And the radio
calls her back from the deep.

The Musical Box

Under its heavy lid, and an inner door of glass,
the brass drum gleams with a million starry spikes.
The grain has lifted, inlay of ship and scroll
sailing away on a sea of ebony,
and the wind rising.

I am six. We kneel on the polar bearskin rug
he brought from the auction, like the box.
He shows me how to lift the glass,
to crank the lever seven times to wind it
and touch the metal wings to set it going.

Fabrique en Genève inside the lid,
brown loops of long-hand, thin up, thick down
and a blot where the nib dipped and squeaked,
Chanson, mazurka, waltz, airs by Verdi and Strauss,
in our living room that fourth summer of war.

I flick the wings with a finger-nail till it spins
to a blur, something alive trapped under ice.
The drum turns slowly, slowly, steel teeth
plucking six tunes from the needles,
one after another, again and again,

and into the rolling wave of the drum
light falls, flattened, with a swish like a skirt,
the click of heels, the echo
of long ago dancing.

Legend

The rooms were mirrors
for that luminous face,
the morning windows ferned
with cold. Outside
a level world of snow.

Voiceless birds in the trees
like notes in the books
in the piano stool.
She let us suck top-of-the-milk
burst from the bottles like corks.

Then wrapped shapeless
we stumped to the park
between the parapets of snow
in the wake of the shovellers,
cardboard rammed in the tines of garden forks.

The lake was an empty rink
and I stepped out,
pushing my sister first
onto its creaking floor.
When I brought her home,

shivering, wailing, soaked,
they thought me a hero.
But I still wake at night,
to hear the Snow Queen's knuckles crack,
black water running fingers through the ice.

The Lace-Maker

A white farm, a black beach
and the long seas running.
At the click of the gate three gulls lift
from the sea and the wind sucks salt, fish
and cat-piss from the old lime-kilns.

She comes between trees to fetch me home,
her apron full of pegs, her lace
cuffing the stones below the waterfall,
pearls beading the air, and in each hand
is one warm egg, laid wild.

Her sheets are out above the field,
tugging for Ireland in a westerly,
billowing slips for pillows and bolsters,
table cloths, petticoats,
angels in lace and clean linen.

She calls, shading her eyes from too much
sea-light, from straining too long, too often
by the wavering light of oil-lamps,
gas-light, a primitive electricity
too frail to stand those wild Atlantic winters,

when at the table she counted her stitches home
in a system of bobbins and beads till every tea
and bed-time were washed in the settled foam
of sea-flowers hooked in a detritus of bird-bones,
her knuckles ivoried with listening.

Women's Work

Their books come with me, women writers,
their verses borne through the rooms
out between the plum trees to the field,
as an animal will gather things,
a brush, a bone, a shoe,
for comfort against darkness.

August Sunday morning,
and I'm casting for words,
wandering the garden sipping their poems,
leaving cups of them here and there in the grass
where the washing steams in the silence
after the hay-days and the birdsong months.

I am sixteen again, and it's summer,
and the sisters are singing, their habits gathered,
sleeves rolled for kitchen work,
rosy hands hoisting cauldrons of greens.
The laundry hisses with steam-irons
glossing the collars of our summer blouses.

Then quietly they go along white gravel,
telling their beads in the walled garden
where *Albertine*'s heady rosaries spill
religious and erotic over the hot stones.
And there's restlessness in the summer air,
like this desire for poems,

our daily offices.

God's Eye

Not long since we threw away the head
filled with fire on All Hallows night,
that lit our suppers
for a week or two.

It lolled on the garden table
till its eye grew moist,
its mouth drooped and we sniffed the air
for putrefaction.

These last days together before Christmas,
as the doors of Advent open,
and every frozen dawn's
a little later,

we sit in our lantern
to see the flame of the rising sun,
a gourd nailed cock-eyed
to the burning tree.

*

The narrowest month and bitter cold.
The moment the house yawns awake
and Earth turns back from the black wastes
of space, dawn breaks its amphora of blood.

We breakfast in our room of glass
to watch the sunrise,
sky overflowing in a cup,
a grapefruit-half in a bowl of gold.

The children sip their juice and gaze
amazed at the gourd of candlefire,
the star in the East so beautiful
it could blind you – like God's eye.

Unpacking the Angel

Twelve papier maché apples
taken one by one
from their dark season in the loft.
Eleven glass balls, one broken.
My children swim to me from their brittle windows.
Birds flown from the mirrors
in the rich house of the lady who asked us to tea
when Dylan was three, and beautiful.

Tangled strands of Woolworths *Lametta*,
saved nearly forty years from a first flat.
Putti from Venice, from the flaking plaster of churches,
from Bellini and Canaletto.
They feather the room like light off water.
The Journey to Bethlehem in brass. The crib
from Tübingen. The Holy Family
I made from *Polyfilla*, wire and rags.

Snarled strings of light bulbs on green flex,
vines of stars, the lights of far-off cities.
From the Christmas fair on the Kürfurstendam
two crystal drops, rousing from the drafts
that stir the tree the whine of air-raids,
the church in flames, stained glass bursting.
And the Berlin angel, whose sleeves still bear
a trace of concrete from the broken wall.

On the twelfth day we undress the tree:
twelve papier maché apples, eleven balls,
ten birds, *Lametta*, putti, painted crib
and Holy Family, the burning city,
angels of mercy and death. All into the box
with flakes of human skin, glitter, glass,
pine-needles sifted to corners and under the flaps,
dust, maybe, from every year of my life.

Snow

The dreamed Christmas,
flakes shaken out of silences so far
and starry we can't sleep for listening
for papery rustles out there in the night
and wake to find our ceiling glimmering,
the day a psaltery of light.

So we're out over the snow fields
before it's all seen off with a salt-lick
of Atlantic air, then home at dusk, snow-blind
from following chains of fox and crow and hare,
to a fire, a roasting bird, a ringing phone,
and voices wondering where we are.

A day foretold by images
of glassy pond, peasant and snowy roof
over the holy child iconed in gold.
Or women shawled against the goosedown air
pleading with soldiers at a shifting frontier
in the snows of television,

while in the secret dark a fresh snow falls
filling our tracks with stars.

December

The dark month
before it can begin again.
The wave hangs in the air
translucent with its cargo
of pebbles, sunlight
and old ship's planks.

We hope for dolphins
suspended in green amber,
a school of porpoise
like a great wheel turning,
a seal heaving ashore,
Excalibur breaking the sea.

The sun skims west
to the edge of the world.
Could that be something
alive in the wave, pulsing
in the mermaid's purse,
in her glittering draperies?

Owl Mythologies

LITTLE OWLS

Was it seven Little Owls last night,
one after another
on the fence-posts of the lane?

Or just the one,
seeing me home
with a stare from every post?

A small, white glare as it stood
bouncing its head in the road,
menacing the car,

then lift-off over the headlights
as it dived away
into the black fields,

coming up for air yards on,
owl on a fence-post,
and again, seven times,

till the last gate
where I slowed into the drive
to the tawny silence of head-lamps going out,

the small gold gaze of the house
and black fields humming
with a quiver of umber wings.

BARN OWL AT LE CHAI

Tonight, cooling off on the terrace,
glow-worms lighting the long grass,
we listen for crickets, nightingales, nightjars,
turning our palms to the first stars.
Little mists rise in the night garden,
then, a shriek of something taken,
and in the darkness under the trees, white
flowers, feathers, her cry in flight,
and the air is blood-flecked,
a grief in retrospect.

SEEING ANGELS

Two in the morning and only the car
in the tunnel of light we made
the whole slow winding way,
our sons' voices on the tape they sent us
played over and over on the mountain roads.

I drown in the black well
and jerk awake from a dream of rain
to the mushroomy smell of forests.
Almost home, raindrops starring the hedge,
village lights beyond the wet black fields.

When you brake on the last hill
there's no thought of angels,
nor a word between us when we see,
feet away, the miraculous hologram
quivering and still as a flame in the wind.

The car's transfixed and purring,
stopped in the small hours by heart-face,
feathers, her talons treading the air.
There's something on the road
trapped by her burning eye.

Holding my breath I step from the car
into the white heat of her hunger.
Hot fur, heartbeat,
two mewing kittens run to my hands,
and the vision's dowsed by the night.

Valley

after glass and slate sculpture by Meical Watts

In water-memory the river turns
always the same way at the boulder
and the bridge.
An ess of current at the land's shoulder,
the falling back of a sleeve where light burns
otter silk below the ridge.

A million million years of water-work
to make this place. A whispering seepage
through lion grass on fire
under snow. A stream's gleaming back
lifts from the mist and marshy weep
as flood meets deep and secret aquifers.

Dwyfor and Glaslyn, green-black rivers of the north
tumbling boulders for the walls of farms,
slip chisels of glass between the slate.
A rumour of ice, flood-fingers in sodden earth.
The bell of an old glacier in the rock's seams
so it splits clean at a tap of light.

Weather works the mountain to the bone
with the let juices of rain, the rising sea's erosion,
a river's gravity, flood's cold reflection,
a valley cut by water over stone.

Into the Mountain

after slate sculpture by Howard Bowcott

1

Sedimentary silt's
slow metamorphosis,
mudstone to shale,
then the squeeze
of the giant's fist.

Light fingers it
with a shimmer like water
on roofscape or slate tip.
A rockface flickers in the wind
as if it moved.

2

Slate to sleep under,
knowing its rain-blue gleam
or the satin of moonlight.
To walk on, cool underfoot,
carrying a tray into the garden

where once Nain stumped in her clogs,
goosefeathers drifting the flags,
and her bucket of water
flung on the dairy floor
ran the gutters blue with milk.

Slabs to set jellies,
cool curds and junkets,
butter slapped to a pattern of oak leaves,
a cheese to be turned,
a beaded jug of milk.

3

His lungs filled
with sediment,
invisible blues, purples,
silty darknesses.
Their branches brimmed
with a shadow of stone
till he couldn't walk, or breathe.
They offered him
a settlement of dust.

4

So slow the strata,
fossils and globules of oil
trapped between pages,
the laying down
of the leaves of slate.

Now, inside mountains,
in the cathedrals of silence,
streams break their beads
into the dark, a fall of vertebrae
too far down to hear.

It begins again,
a fall of earth.
Between history's pages
they will find the body of a man
like a fern.

Layers of Melancholy

after wood sculpture by Michael Fairfax

1

In the beached boat
the fall of the tree

in the creak of the rigging
the swelling forest

in the petrified stumps at low tide
the rustling seasons

in the charred wood
the sigh of flame

in the dark wing of a bird
the long migrations

in the labia of burnt oak
the slow centuries

in the acorn's drop
the shadow

2

A time when on their daily walk
she made a small pause on the lane
and looked back to that house
where they'd lived so easily for years.

Then, in the shadow of the fallen oak,
she thought she saw a wrong she'd seen before
elsewhere, years back,
let in like a cat from the dark.

At once the track seemed stonier,
the heat of the day savage.
He, smiling at the turn, stood then
under the dangerous pendulum of the sun.

He was too far away
and she couldn't call or run
as if she'd slipped between the wafers of light
into another time, the wrong road taken.

Behind, like the shifting perspective of woods,
their house was a house of glass, and she,
salt-still on the track, with the grief of trees
wept in the brittle air.

European Field

an installation by Anthony Gormley

Thirty-five thousand faces in a field
the colour of clay and flesh and blood
crammed between clean white walls of a gallery.
Thirty-five thousand on tip-toe
craning their necks
breathing like a field of corn.

Thirty-five thousand voices asking
why, why, why
like wind in the grasses
of graveyards and old battlefields.
Seventy thousand ears listening
to no answer.

We have paid to see them.
We did not expect to be stared at,
or that they would move in to live with us,
taking root in the field of our minds,
whispering all night
'we are you, you, you.'

Thirty-five thousand figures
crumbling in my head
to bones and dust and ashes
under a field of flowering grasses.

The Paddle Steamers

In the great grey tank of the rising sea
muscular river and sea-currents flex
and the Severn's wrestle of waters
cracks two shores open.

Dawn a quiver on a bedroom ceiling
and it's quick, up and away,
with bread and cheese, windfalls
and dandelion burdock,
the flash of clean white daps on the pedals.

Drop a bike on the stones,
step under the echoing cold of the pier,
pick lapis blue mussels and amberweed necklaces
from the terrible stanchions of rust,
wait for the paddle steamer rounding the headland.

Sometimes it was me in the prow
of *Glen Usk, Ravenswood, The Cardiff Queen*,
waves oiling apart to port and starboard,
light a slither of water-snakes,
a whiplash of metals and mermaid hair.

The tide recedes, taking its time.
Away it slides over the mud-flats
leaving a gleam of pebbles, crustacea, driftwood,
and a rusty bicycle without wheels.

Light

Lit windows in the dark,
the intimacy of rooms,
sofas, photographs,
the flicker of television.

Sometimes a twinkling city
beyond the windows of a train,
or camp-fires of desert nomads
seen from a plane
and mountain villages winking in the passes.

Then that baby-memory of the hurt town
where every night was black and the sky
broke into something called peace,
a hundred war-planes with their glad-rags on
strafing the town with light.

My father opened blackout curtains,
switched all the lights on,
and house after house across Europe
set fire to the dark.

Tonight, just a scatter of farm-lights,
and the wandering torch of a plane
like a watchman's lamp
between the crackling stars.

Hafod

Frail architecture, its fine lines razed
from the tangled pleasure grounds below the ridge,
where the idea of a house is stronger
than walls, a fallen roof, temple and bridge.
Even the waterfall, Laporte's engraving
or the real thing after heavy rain, reflects
stonework and windows of a house
turned to a memory of the picturesque
young Turner painted; or Coleridge, passing this way
from Devil's Bridge over the mountain track,
astonished, perhaps, by a glimpse of Xanadu
one afternoon two hundred summers back.

Here Thomas Johnes' dream grew tall,
the wilderness flowering in his mind
while the carriage stumbled the stony road from Hereford.
The last twelve miles on foot in rain and wind,
driven by visions of a great estate
rising above the river under Pumlumon,
his mountains clothed in larch and oak and ash,
three million reddening in late November sun.
Jane's lists remain, her smugglers' silks,
four kinds of lace, muslin for an apron,
her twenty yards of ribbon for a bonnet.
'Brocaded silk,' she wrote, 'are all the tone.'

All gone, but the idea of quiet rooms,
the octagon library under its cupola
where he worked late on ancient manuscripts,
their words flickering under the candelabra.
The end of the line. The bright young naturalist,
Mariamne, beloved only child,
dead at twenty-seven. His fortune spent, a house and a class
in ruins, the gardens turned back to the wild.
Under mulch a flake of gold, a marbled skull,
a peacock's feather in the grass, shadows
that could be the disposition of a house,
each fall a myth of sun-reflecting windows.

The City

THE JOURNEY

A four-hour drive through geological time,
to the two blue notes of the cuckoo: C and A flat
again and again from oak woods sweet with bluebells
as if it sang the scent and colour of blue.

And in my mind a sedimentary language,
words laid down on the mind's bedrock, names
remembered from an old geography book:
Ordovician flags, shales, mudstones,
Silurian shale, grit, greywacke, limestone
formed from crushed fossils, dead reefs
of coral, and the petrified stems of sea lilies
from warm and long retreated shallow seas;
Cambrian slate that once roofed the nation;
the coal-bearing shales and limestones of the Dee,
where my grandfather farmed stony land
and milled his corn to the west of Offa's Dyke.

Over the Manchester Ship Canal,
over Irwell, Medlock, Tame and Irk,
braided streams of Celtic and Old English,
into the ancient Kingdom of Elmet where
Celts fell to Angles in the last lost battle.

Names from the radio: Barbirolli, Hallé, Cantona,
Old Trafford, Moss-side, The Manchester Ship Canal:
enough to wake from the page of a child's atlas,
dreams of the somewhere else we long to go:
the imagined floating city, like a barge
drifting in green waters to the sea.

Mamucium, a Roman fort at the breast,
a sandstone bluff where Irwell and Medlock meet
under the watershed of gritstone moors
and the limestone peaks of Derbyshire,
Victoria's rose-red city built on muck and brass.

Listen! to the pentameters of weather,
the 'deep depressions moving from the west',
'the M6 hazardous with surface water',
as fronts surfing the waves of the weatherman's map
break on a city famous for its rain;
Listen to the monosyllables of stone,
where mountains become fells, and valleys, dales,
craig is *bluff*; *afon* and river and stream,
are *beck* and *gill*; a waterfall's a *force*.

And history: cotton and coal.
The oscillating beat of the looms' drum
under the singing water of the fells,
that built a city out of terracotta,
faience, stone and brick, great warehouses
beautiful and boastful as cathedrals,
and terraced back-to-backs where poverty,
filth and cholera flourished under the smoke
that wreathed the city with poisons, and with power.

For Empire. For profit. For cotton.
And the century of toxins and disease
was in full spate. The map of the world
stained with the colour of possession, the air
venomous. The planet will begin to die.

*

The century of trade and manufacture
was just 'history', stories my father told me.
The cotton against our skin and on our beds
came raw from India on ships he sailed in,
long before I was born, young radio officer
berthing at Liverpool, Southampton, Cardiff,
on the great merchant ships that plied the trade-routes.
I never thought of the cost of it.

Clean cotton over goosedown, cloud-deep beds.
Cotton my mother stitched, turning the sheets
end to middle, eking out the threadbare
precious stuff brought damp from the garden
with the sun and the wind in it. The smell of it

hot from the ironing board, folded crisp
as envelopes, or peach-skinned flannelette
to tuck a child in, safe as a parcel,
before I knew about the smoke, the dust,
the noise, the poverty, the rows of back-to-back.

*

My mother in the '30s, a country girl,
bright daughter of a North Wales tenant farmer,
learning the midwife's art in the slums of Salford,
delivered babies on filthy mattresses,
with nothing but old newspapers for sheets
and not a shovel of coal for the grate.

She'd shared a bed with sisters, been forced to hide
in the hay-loft from her brothers for some peace
to read a book, never had anything new,
wore sisters' too big hand-me-downs and make-do's,
fed the animals and fetched the eggs,
then walked ten miles to the Grammar School.

After homework by oil-lamp light, she helped her mother
churn butter for a family of twelve.
She saw beasts born in meadow-grass, carried
new-born lambs to a shippon and clean straw.
Her supper was stoneground bread and buttermilk.
She slept to the sound of water turning the mill-wheel,
and thought that poverty.

Now, in the city she'd dreamed of,
she saw human babies slither into life
to die, or to be motherless, taken
by the plagues of poverty and filth.

*

And in my time, long ago black and white tragedies,
the football heroes dead in the plane crash,
the fires, the riots, the horror of Saddleworth moor.

*

Then the thesaurus of cloth:
Bolts and reels of cloth, the woof and weft
of batiste and broadcloth, calico, cambric, crêpe,
challis, cheesecloth, chintz, organdie, muslin,
serge for businessmen, worsted for workers,
the foulard, fustian, flannel, surah, ticking and drill.

For smoothness and sheen: crêpe satin, peau de soie,
damask for the tables of great houses,
spread with silver, porcelain and crystal.
For opulence: brocade, chenille, sateen,
tapestry, velvet, plush.
Stockport, biggest bowler hat factory in the world.
Mills up country on the Yorkshire moors
spun nothing but black silk for widows.

And the warehouses, red-brick magnificence,
safe-guarding riches to trade with the world,
whose profits would raise mansions in the suburbs,
and fill the city with banks and counting-houses,
temples to non-conformism, the work-ethic, thrift;
would lay down railways, build viaducts, canals,
lure the rural poor from the Lancashire fells,
from Wales and Ireland to work the mills,
to full, spin, dye, weave, cut,
to tailor and sell cloth to the world. And lads,
whose sisters were in service to the rich,
came from the South Wales valleys, from quarry, pit
and mountain farm to learn the clothing trade,
made good, went home to open haberdasheries
and draper's shops called *Manchester House*
in little towns from Pwllheli to Pontypridd.

*

The children of poverty were tough, grew up,
worked, or not, in the teeming web of
the red rose and the white, the Saxon and the Celt,
of those who migrated to the city from west
and east, to make a city rich and various
in language, accent, song and dance and habit
the culinary arts, the rites of passage,

brass band, parade, eisteddfod, ceilidh, carnival.
The Whitsun Walk, the Corpus Christi procession.
The anthems and flags of difference to be shared,
the red and the green, the dragon and Union Jack.

They quarrelled, got drunk, prayed to many gods,
grew restive in their chains and lost their histories
in the century's confusion. Till here we are
at the end of the millennium, beginning again
on a geological fault, holding our breath
for peace, to see a music palace built on bedrock.

THE CONCERT HALL

Walk Deansgate from the Cathedral – to Castlefield,
Roman Fort at the confluence of Irwell
and Medlock, where moody warehouses reflect
on the silent cloudy waters of canals.

Close by, where road and rail and waterway
tangle above the tribal waters, ravelled
and unravelled by engineers, bridged,
culverted, lost and found again, they built
a hall over sandstone, over the spaces between us,
over the strata, over the races and the tribes,
the rifts of history. A hall for the harp and the bard,
as on this very ground, fifteen centuries ago,
in the courts of the kings of Elmet, there was a place
for music and poetry to praise, lament,
to celebrate, name and number us,
to tell us who we are and sing the world
alive. A hall for music like a great boast.

Once fields were here, crossed by a lost tributary
of the river Tib. Built over, fallen to dereliction
and parked cars. Soon there were cranes and scaffolding,
on acres of crushed rubble within sight
of Lutyens' elegant cenotaph for the dead

of the Great War, *The Britons Protection*, pulling
pints, defiant among the demolition gangs,
Metrolink, the railway, and the Rochdale canal.
The Midland Hotel where Mr Rolls met Mr Royce.

When they've counted the JCBs, the pile-drivers,
the yellow cranes, the crushed Victorian brick-dust,
the cubic metres of concrete, the columns and beams,
the seven thousand high-strength grip bolts,
the scaffolding poles that would reach from here to Hull,
the fifteen springs under every one of the columns
buoyed over bedrock of sandstone and Manchester marl,
the stainless steel ribs channelling rain from the roof,

When they've constructed the silent underworld
of air-conditioning, suspended the auditorium
ceiling in webbed steel in a tension of struts,
nodes and tie-rods, the slight twist in the slabs
to diffuse the least flicker of leftover sound,
and raised a branch of yew on the summit of the roof
to appease the gods of the ancient forests,

When the artists have hung their delicate white veils,
their rippling ribbons of metal running with colour,
and the sculptor caressed the fold of a swelling wave
in his enormous egg of Carrara marble
balanced so lightly on the palm of the earth.

Then the hall floats on its springs above the ground,
a perfect instrument for listening.

VOICING THE ORGAN

He must voice the organ. Twenty two tons of machine
must be taught to whisper like teaching a glacier to thaw.
Over the sea from Aabenraa, each pipe
hand-planed and sanded to silk, swell-boxes, windchests
of pine, their secret interiors stroked like skin.
Hand-carved rods. Oak and cherry, rosewood,

mahogany, walnut, ebony, each in its place.
Four winter months he works with thousands of pieces
like the puzzle of bones of a whale from the permafrost
that has forgotten its song.

He voices the whale, works in the silent nights,
the auditorium deaf to the cries of the city.
He listens, head cocked as the thrush on the lawn, his touch
so light, stroking and easing, till all pipes in a rank,
all notes in a stop sing with the same timbre,
all seventy-six stops with their beautiful names,
Principal, Octave, Quint and Cornet,
Voix Celeste, Voix Humaine, celestial and human,
a perfect choir, as if voicing the organ had given it a soul.

For the first time after the ice, the high notes,
first drops out of silence, then the beginning
of trickling, the beginning of streams, rivers,
then thundering torrents and the wind roaring over the ice.
And with the thaw the pain must begin,
the cry of an earth that's alive again.

As they switch on the lights in the steel web of the ceiling,
five thousand pipes will gleam in a breaking wave
of steel. The audience will come, taking their places
with a collective murmur of pleasure, the house lights dim,
the organist arrive, the first notes sound in the hush.
And the anonymous man who listened late
into winter nights for the accent of every stop,
who voiced it in the silence of the night,
will be somewhere else, letting it go.

THE BOMB

On that June day, not one of the workmen labouring
in the hush of the Bridgewater Hall heard the explosion
that stopped the city in its tracks, before it hurt,
like news of grief suddenly reaching the heart.

Saturday, 15th of June, at 10 in the morning.
With her two thumbs a woman tests the fontanel
of a melon for ripeness. A girl tries on a dress.
A couple buy a cot in Mothercare.
In Smiths people flick through paperbacks.
In the Cathedral someone without hope
kneels down to say so, hoping to be heard.
In the Corn Exchange old things in the antique shops
survived the blitz in the corners of front rooms,
a clock still ticking after ninety years,
porcelain and mahogany that graced
grand houses in the heyday of the city.
The lovely theatre in the Royal Exchange
waits in the morning's pause for something to happen.
An ice cream parlour, a tobacconist, a bistro,
jewellers, boutiques, a Costume Hire Centre,
shops and stalls, offices, Carcanet Press,
where poetry's quiet, compressed in the book's pages
and phones and computers are taking the day off.

Then the bomb. The moment hangs in the air.
People stand stone still in the frozen city.
The woman with the melon remembers her child,
and rushes away without paying, the fruit held
like a precious bowl in her hands. In Mothercare
the couple look at each other, and the foetus drifts
in its shallow sea like a sea lily tugging its stem.

Then chaos, before the two blue notes of terror.

In that moment of frozen time, plate glass
buckles before it blows. Brickwork bulges
and is slowly taken apart, Lego-Town
swept to smithereens by a child's petulance.

Glass hangs in the air, scarves, tee shirts,
flowers, newspapers, Kleenex, polythene bags,
migrating flocks of birds of paradise,
and real birds, city doves and sparrows
flung from the centre of violence, torn and bloody,
and paper rafts from shattered offices
set off like pretty ships across the sky.

On the palm of a ledge outside the publisher's window
in the Corn Exchange is a clutch of broken eggs,
fledglings blown away twig-limbed and goggle-eyed.
I imagine a poem of love from the publisher's desk
afloat like a bright balloon against the wire.

*

Bring out the road-sweepers. Wash the city in rage.
Bring builders and scaffolders, bricklayers, carpenters, shop-fitters.
Bring on the pavement artists and the street players.
Bring the fiddler with coins in his cap, and the lonely saxophonist,
the sandwich-board born-again Christian who says:
'*Your Sins Be Forgiven.*' Bring out *The Big Issue*,
the singer and the poet. Let them sing in the city.
Let them build a music-house where just to be human
is to be washed by pleasure, and grief, and rage.
Let them build a bridge over water.
Bring on the 'cello and the piccolo.
Let the organ sound.

Concerto

Poem in four movements

PIAZZA

Stillness of stone in the street, Yasuda's monolith
asleep on limestone, white marble veined with silver.
Flesh not yet born, limbless in its caul of pearly skin.
I touch it every day for a week, and last thing
at night, lean from my window in the Midland Hotel,
electric with vertigo over the perilous street,
to see it motionless under the moon. At dawn
it's still there. Why hasn't it lolloped away
into the water, and found its way home to the sea?

*

The children dance on the piazza
and tell tall tales about the stone:
animal, egg, thing from the depths of the sea.
They're giddy at the very sight of it,
two hundred thousand pounds worth of Fine Art.

In their dreams they crack it open for its soul,
sleeping beast, its paws and head tucked in.
They would tame Carrara marble, caress,
cajole and cuddle it, lay their cheeks against its skin.
They piggy-back each other up its flanks
then slither off as if, in its marble sleep,
it stirred, skin twitching, like an old horse.

'Look! Men are carrying past a sun and a moon.'
Sure enough, there in the street, borne
down the pavement like shop-fitters' accessories,
to be hoisted into the sky on the hook of a crane,
sun and moon to dangle above the heads
of the street-musicians. Soon the piazza is dancing
a one-foot jig to the beat of the drums.

Under a sparkling umbrella in the hot mid-day sun
in his black-tie and tails and his high-shine shoes, the dancing man
leads his little band along the street. They cross the road
among the traffic, music their lollipop man.
Drivers wind their windows down and wait,
tapping a tune on the steering wheel.

The streets are a dazzle of day-glo police jackets,
drummers, magicians, stilt-walkers, jugglers and jazz.
A child strokes the velvet muzzle of a police horse,
and it prances delicately like part of the show.
Radio's loud and live in Albert Square,
and the sky's adrift with balloons going westwards
and upwards trailing their strings over the holiday city,
trailing their pebble shadows over the grounded stone.

FOYER

Inside the concert hall, in the walls of glass,
the public spaces tremble with water-light.
Shadows and reflections run on silent looms.
Healey's metal ribbons ripple like flame,
like water falling four floors down, beneath
the undercliff of the wall. Their secret surfaces
of silver, red and blue reflect on white.
His theme, the broken threads of the cotton trade.
His flying shuttles of light pick up a seed,
a wing, a raindrop, a ripple, a pigeon alighting
on the pavement, a flight of balloons, the flash of a car mirror,
the burning sky, to make a river of steel,
to make a weir of turbulent colour that dashes
the coldness of white architectural space.

Against glass, over the canal,
where three mallards float in their water rings,
Kate Egan's 'Space Piece' hangs its sky-map
picked out in a scatter of blue plastic price tags,
broken ripples of comets on floating white,

hemmed and weighted down by riveted braid
for the hems of jeans. Airy hangings that net
the sifted linens of light, the muslins of mist,
sunlit water falling straight to the earth, like rain.

UNDERCROFT

For a week I live in a concert hall,
mouse in the shadows, watcher and listener,
like a lesser bard skirting the edge of the court,
lest my harping trouble the king.

Down flights of stairs into the underworld,
underfoot, under floor, in the silent spaces
of the undercroft, the building treads on springs,
resting its weight a wafer above ground.
To prove it, a blade of light off the canal
slides in to flicker under suspended walls.

Slopes and outcrops of a real earth
underlie gravel and aggregate, the ghost
of world under world. Paths wind through glades of concrete.
Overhead the pipework is lagged in silver
dragon skin. Vast air-conditioning pipes
like the husk of a great instrument,
taking the sighs and hurricanes of human breath
slowly and soundlessly away. In there is
the breath that made the note that broke your heart,
and the gasp you gave as you listened to it.

After the next Ice Age, should giants with snow feet
inhabit the earth, they could lift this building,
held to the ground by nothing but gravity.
One at each corner, they would trundle it off
under a dust-cloth, like a concert piano
after the concerto, leaving behind
only a pebble of Carrara marble
and a mysterious henge of a hundred
and forty six concrete pillars, all
that remains of a strange religion.

A petrified forest, the occasional haunt
of the maintenance man with the spanner.
This is pantomime practising the art
of perspective, the enchanted thicket, not quite
convincing trees, a path into silence
webbed with shadows.

The furniture is under sheets.
No one dines at the water table.
Nothing's alive here but an insect,
a winged thing on the gravel,
waving its feelers in the white forest.

Imagine a trapped bird, thrush
or nightingale singing on a branch
deep in the thicket in fluorescent twilight.
Or the sound of a 'cello, playing
for Persephone lost in the underworld,
for Demeter whose sorrow locked the earth in winter.
Her underworld of grief is this: not fire,
but drifts of sifting snow.

*

Underground, not so far away,
perhaps along this very seam of sandstone,
tapping their message to the universe
in the path of the planned airport runway,
the tunnellers with their banners and barricades,
voice the people's instinct against the machine
as their ancestors did when they smashed the looms.

AUDITORIUM

The doors are shut on the jewelled inner sanctum
where maestro and the virtuoso practise their secret arts
in the alchemistry of music.

*

I know a gate between fields
that sings five notes in the wind,
a scale or a random air.
Sometimes the wind breathes
through the pipes in such a way
that I'm transfixed
by the sorrow in a sound,
and lay my ear to the gate
to possess it.

Is that how music began?
A woman singing in a cave
to the airs of the sea
as if it's inside her?
A man in a forest
hearing the arrow's song
fly to the stag's heart
right through his own?

*

High in the gallery
I creep through fired bronze doors
into the graded earth-colours
of the pleasure palace,
an illicit listener in the shadows
to look down on the orchestra
rehearsing Elgar in trainers and jeans,
astride their 'cellos, nestling violins
against their cheeks, stroking
the double bass to a deep purr,
tonguing the flute.

*

Down the levels. Past doors that read
Maestro, Guest Conductor, Leader.
In the kitchen a shopping list scrawled
on a door is a legend: Star Nozzles,
Fine Chinou, Ramekins, Skull caps.

*

The auditorium lolls, rumpled, between rehearsals,
the players at break. A stepladder stands in the aisle,
the stage is a scatter of chairs and music-stands.
Only the organist, divested of the golden cloak
she wore for the recital, hands on the keys, head bowed,
listens for a fall of silence before the first note.

*

I am under the organ,
inside it, unseen,
stealing her music,
my fingers in the honey.
I lean on the wall,
dizzied by the humming.
The great engine vibrates.
It purrs under my finger tips.
Its breathing strokes my bones
as if I were a violin,
and runs to the heart like shock.
I am between the dragon's paws.
I have become the instrument.
Like a gate with the wind in it.

*

They cross the pavement, touching the stone as they pass.
There is time for a drink, to greet friends, buy a programme.
They weave under the wall of colour and drift in
to find their seats and settle and let pleasure
begin its alchemy. There is a building
to be appraised, talked about, gazed at.
Latecomers unsettle them. They must rise
awkwardly, not quite standing up, their things
spill from their laps. The auditorium walls
are dark and rich as earth. The ceiling
is starlight. Microphones dangle on gossamers
over the space. In the perfect musical box
of the hall even the hum of chatter
seems rich and deep as a hive. Behind the stage
tonight, the organ's a frozen waterfall
that might never have thawed,
never hummed in my bones.

Every instrument begins to speak. Every string
is touched. Every note is sounded.
A random babble of gossiping strings and brass
is a market-place of sound, a cacophony,
without art, or meaning. But it promises
everything, is suddenly composed.

The dancing conductor on his podium
ignites the orchestra, the choir, the audience,
the angel boy who sings his heart out
under the starry heaven of the ceiling.
The conductor's white cuff flutters, a trapped moth
in the polished mirror of a chandelier lamp.
His wand is summer lightning. His feet dance
on the stage, his fingers touch the ceiling.

*

The soprano as blonde and small as a child,
reaches a note so sweet and high
she is more than human.

*

Skin listens. Fingers vibrate on the arm rests.
A chord plays in the heart.
The 'cello strokes the bones.
We become the instrument.

If we wait long enough,
maybe the giants will come
to carry the hall away,
and we'll believe the music was a dream.

*

In the interval the audience walk out.
They talk and queue and take the air.
With the music still in our minds
we're too tender to say too much
so the talk is small.
The stone on the piazza is an ice cube

in a glass. It drowns in the mist of chilled wine.
A month from midsummer,
and the sky still blue in the long evening light.
The pavement beggar asks for our small change.
The city glows in the last light of the sun.
Glass walls are touched by its baton of fire.

Because of the music, tonight we will all be changed.
When it's over, the auditorium empty,
I'll think of the organ's ghost in the undercroft,
and the stone in the white stare of the moon,
in thrall to each other's gravity, like love.

Horse Goddess

for Catrin

As a child she'd canter the yard astride a stick
topped by the stuffed sack of a horse's head
haltered with knotted hemp.
She fed it apples and fists of grass.
At night she'd stable it
in a corner of her sleep.

When she grew strong, tall as her brothers,
she built a dancer from the bones of horses
from the knackers yard, scraped and bleached them,
wove them into limbs, the spine and thighs
of Atalanta running, set the scoured skull
of a horse between the shoulders –

– like the head of *Equus Caballus* brought from the thaw
of the million-year-old glacier.
She strung horse-woman from the studio ceiling,
a giantess who leaped in the bone light
and shadow-danced on walls where the sea shook,
and you heard the hoof and heart-beats of dead horses.

She slept four nights in a stable waiting
for the foal. Asleep, awake, asleep again
in the dark stall. Outside frost bit the fields.
Pond and bucket brimmed with icy stars.
In the mare the foetus drifted on its stem,
treading water in the blood-warm dark.

On the fourth night the mare began to steam,
filled the barn with sweat like the land of Dyfed
trapped in the enchantment of a mist.
The mare, lumbering through waves of labour,
licked and nuzzled inanimate things
mad with longing for her foal.

She stiffened, threw back her head
not breathing for a long moment.
Then, a hoof from the waters, a small muzzle
shaking itself with a sneeze out of the caul,
slipped flipping like a landed fish,
first footing it into the world.

Balancing

for George Dewez

'A question of balance,' he said,
leaning the small weight of his body
against the air. Beneath the press of his thigh
the mare stepped away, hoof over delicate hoof,
catching his weight again.

She did it perfectly, as if
concentrating, or listening
to a beat deeper than music,
tacking the seas of her brain
under gravity's shifting centre.

And somewhere in horse-memory
out there under the moon
a stallion danced hoof over hoof
before the sleepy mares,
his blood on fire.

Stamping starlight from wet grass,
he turned the planet under his hooves,
as the moon inched west,
drawing the sea's veined silver
like a horse's skin.

Sloes

The year he died, never so many mushrooms,
and sloes blue in their crowns of thorns.
Day after day we were out gathering,
cramming jars, stowing the freezer,

till the house was a spice-box of eastern names,
ginger, cinnamon, vanilla, star anise,
in their aromatic syrups. Baskets
filled with fungi, plushy, pink-gilled,

too many to eat, lifted from the morning
grass, warm as new eggs.
The best steamed in butter. The rest
darkened in the fridge to a musky rot.

The children picked the sloes, out
so long I stood, uneasy,
folding clothes from the line,
calling their names over the fields.

They ran up the lane with their jewels,
their hands and faces stained with juice,
the enamel-blue bloom of the thorn-fruit
blackening with their finger prints.

Months passed him by, his gold ring
loosening on his finger. That winter,
when the gin was dark as blood
and turned us tipsy, he had gone.

We kept one bottle longer than the rest,
forgot it in the back of the cupboard,
and found it, tidying up, uncorked it,
and wondered at the taste of shadows in it.

Green Man

for Tony Conran

In your library I could have sworn I heard
the rustle of ferns rooting in deep crevasses,
the crackle of spores, a gasp of melting snow.
High-ledged among the spines of Yeats, R.S., Sorley,
the Mabinogi's streams, wilderness greened
in the stagnant water of jars.
Hart's Tongue. Lemon-scented. Maidenhair.

Later, that wet midsummer night – never mind
the rain – you made me climb your mountain garden,
a bit of pre-Cambrian tamed by the suburb.
The two of us tottered up, up in a stumble
through a drench of ferns and sweet mock orange,
and turned to see the glittering run of the Straits.
Polypody. Adder's Tongue. Brake.

I squint through a glass at the flipside of ferns – ovaries,
seed-sacs along each backbone like roe.
Like your poet's hands that stole the public road
for rhododendron and scented azalea,
spored with gold-dust as the pages of old books
for the making of poems, gardens, daughters.
Male fern. Lady Fern. Moonwort.

Estuary

The sea was light
before the dazzle of the empty page
and the window flashed across the bay

Stones were jewellery
before pebbles grew dry in our pockets
and died on our window-sills

Water and stone were calligraphy
before ogham and ink,
before words came like birds to our screens

Driftwood was forest before the timberman,
the sawyer, the shipwright, the fishing boat
lost with all hands in the October sea

Skies were thunder
before jets cracked clouds
before the rent skin of sound

River and tide wrestled
and heron was all the colours of grey
before the salmon leaped in feathers and spray

and with heavy wings the bird made off
with the sky on its back,
and the sea in its beak.

Lines on First Hearing . . .

Suddenly, on a silent gardening day,
two notes from half a mile away.

Did we hear it? Too far, too deep
in trees heaving their bones from sleep

to be quite sure. Again. A bird's voice.
C and A flat. Treacherous sweetness

in two clear notes across the valley's well
of silence and the winds of April.

We set our tools aside and listen hard
to hear it calling from the leafless wood,

excited once more by a summer guest
who pitches camp in a small bird's plundered nest,

grows fat on murder, and in a stolen house
rehearses two notes in an angel's voice.

Letters from Bosnia

Wales spelt *Vales*
on the brown envelope
from Vites to Llanidloes.
Inside a bundle of pages,
little illuminated manuscripts
of gilded Easter eggs,
scenes from a European spring
we'd all know anywhere,
an afternoon's work from the class in Vites.
'Dear Ben,' says one,
'You are my friend. Write me. Misha.'

Quietly, heads bent over the pages,
the children write the first draft of a poem.
Outside April is all indecision,
daffodils over, lawns blurred with speedwell,
the cherries torn by a sharp rain.
In the photograph, yesterday's Misha is smiling.
A class group grinning, pulling faces.
They wave, thumbs up to the future.
Behind them, in the rendered wall of the school
are the bullet holes.

At L'Oursinado

for David

Waves beating on white stone,
and a wind from Africa.
On the terrace under the pines,
the waiter shakes a white cloth
out over the table and the sea.

Bringing news of a tempest
treading the Mediterranean from the south,
he lifts the bottle in its coif
and pours a stuttering gleam of wine
into the night.

We sip saffron and fish, the slow glamour of rosé.
A hot wind shakes our tent of shadows,
sings in the mouths of wine-glasses.
Silvers run in from the sea to earth
in the cordons of our wrists.

The night is dangerous,
the car winces on the open road.
We shutter and bolt the Tower,
roping our bed to the earth and lie
in the stirred scent of rosemary.

Forest and wind fold
or will break each other.
The white room luminous with static
flinches electric all night on a wild sea
and the mountains rumbling.

In the morning lion breathes.
There's a shaking of manes,
the wet pelt of wilderness.
I peg out a sheet
to fill with the breathing of trees.

Wherever we cast white cotton into a room
to fall, settling, on a bed,
it will glimmer with lightnings,
clean linen gathered from the air
dry and crumpled as a wind from Africa.

Magdalene in Provence

for Santa Raymond

S.R.: 'Do you believe the story that Mary Magdalene spent her last years here?'
Nun at Sainte Baume: 'I don't know if she was here then, but she's here now.'

1

In mid-day heat we take the precipitous road
to Gémenos. Over a succulent valley
we pause in scents of pine and bergamot,
and all day the car brims with musk and honey.

Below, the sound of water, a quick stream,
cedars of Lebanon, a Judas tree,
and, red-gold under cliffs, like an old moment
of faith in wilderness, a quiet abbey.

On the secret forest path, where water fans
its moonlight over limestone, two girls spread
a scarlet carpet on the rock. They scrub
under falling water, till the stream runs red.

Original sin flows with us through the woods
all the way back to the car like a stain of blood.

2

It's cold on the Col de L'Espigoulier.
Cloud darkens the mountains. There's rain in the air.
At Sainte Baume the rain sets in, we're hungry,
the restaurant closed, lunch finished everywhere.

An old man shivers over a stall of gourds
bright in the drizzle. A red earth track
leads into the mist between fields of fennel.
We've come so far now, there's no turning back.

Fleece jackets over summer things, sandals,
one waterproof, a National Trust umbrella.
In the loneliness of rain, no one
will watch our pilgrimage. We swallow

grapes, chocolate, a little bread and wine,
and walk between the hawthorns and the pines.

3

The forest is huge with silence. No birds sing.
Two hours ascending the broken stairs
of fallen stone and root, under the oaks
cathedral-high and holy in the dank air

where nothing is alive but quiet roots,
one sorrowful magpie chances a cry,
and a woodpecker yaffles in the shocked hush
away among the branching clerestories.

Yews a thousand years old, and oak and beech
seeded from trees that were seeded from trees
that grew when she sucked wild honey from the comb,
sipped dew collected in the cups of leaves,

and kept herself alive on fruit and roots,
and lions lay down on the path and licked her feet.

4

God knows where this will end,
stairs made for pilgrims out of stone and root,
under the hanging curtains of the rain,
soaked to the skin, soaked to the heart in doubt.

Our sandals fill with pine needles and grit,
rain channels down the ditch of my spine.
My skin is limestone, my sweat a cloud
rising in milky light through the wild vines.

Then a bell, clean, watery and far away,
a mountain bell, its iron hollowness
augmented by the curved, cave-hollowed limestone
of the ridge, human hands ringing the Angelus,

two hands that rub themselves as she turns away
from the shaking rope, murmuring the rosary.

5

We should be afraid. Alone, I'd welcome company
of lion or wolf to lead the way. Huge boulders
blackened by moss mark the track's corners,
dumb, eyeless presences, their shoulders

hunched in damp. We hurry past to a flight
of proper steps and the Stations of the Cross,
a shop with chocolate bars and rosaries,
a vast candlelit cave gleaming with brass, gross

nineteenth-century marble, meaty Christs,
crude modern glass that bloodies the air.
I wipe them from my mind, remember it was here
she lived out her last years with Maximin – her fabled hair

grown grey as mist under the aisles of trees,
the steady falling rain, her history.

6

Something keeps fear at bay as we slither down,
hand in hand, listening for the tread
of a woman and a big cat on the path
under the dripping trees. But the forest is dead.

Home to the Tower. Sky cracks awake
with electricity, the mountains growl,
all rooms shuttered but one to watch
the storm, the animals of darkness prowl.

Home to a fire of olive wood, a hot bath strewn
with rosemary, warmed towels, a glass of wine,
clean sheets, a box of spikenard to break
over your sunburnt, rain-chilled skin, and mine,

to lie listening to thunder shake the land,
licking wild honey from each other's hands.

Language Act

Eisteddfod 1993

We watch ourselves on television in the rain,
disputing our language in the other tongue.
The government messenger, come to view
the picturesque, is caught in the storm
under downpouring skies.

People we know, friends, acquaintances,
point at the ruddy Saxon face,
and have their say.
We lip-read his curses
bleeped from the soundtrack.

By now he'll be on the motorway,
or in the easing glow of the hotel,
towelling rain from his yellow hair,
shaking off the words like bees,
picking the stings from his skin.

We switch off the news, listen
to the rain falling fluent, filling
the Bwdram, the Glowan and the Clettwr,
finding its tongue in the ancient dark
of the deepest aquifers.

Translation

after translating from Welsh, particularly a novel by Kate Roberts

Your hand on her hand – you've never been
this close to a woman since your mother's beauty
at the school gate took your breath away,
since you held hot sticky hands with your best friend,
since you, schoolgirl guest in a miner's house,
two up, two down, too small for guest rooms
or guest beds, shared with two sisters,
giggling in the dark, hearts hot with boy-talk.

You spread the script. She hands you a fruit.
You break it, eat, know exactly how
to hold its velvet weight, to bite, to taste it
to the last gold shred. But you're lost for words,
can't think of the English for *eirin* – it's on the tip of your –
But the cat ate your tongue, licking peach juice
from your palm with its rough *langue de chat*,
tafod cath, the rasp of loss.

The Vision of Piers Plowman

by William Langland (14th century)

a version

PASSUS XI

My dreams were troubled, then Nature came,
woke me and called me by my name.
'Come with me. Learn what the wilderness is worth.'
So he led me to the mountain, Middle-Earth.

There I saw the sun shining on sea and land
where untamed creatures couple with their kind:
the wild wood-snakes, birds in the forest cover
in the bright fleck and flicker of their feathers,
while human pairs in poverty and plenty,
in peace, in war, in joy and misery,
grasp greedily for gold and show no pity.

Yet the wild beasts, so wise, so steady,
feed, drink, pair and birth their young.
After the heat, the rut and strut of mating
male keeps sad company with male
and leaves his mate alone all night and day.
No cow in calf would bellow for the bull,
nor hind for stag, nor lioness for lion when she's full
with young. Nor would the boar
lust after the sow, nor stallion for mare,
nor dog for bitch, nor cat for queen, nor cock for hen.
Once he has kindled her with kittens, calf, foal, fawn,
no wild animal would meddle with its mate.

A bird builds in the thicket a house so intricate.
The magpie stitches sticks for a cunning nest
then lays her eggs and warms them with her breast.
No plasterer could wattle a wall so well,
no mason's stone is dressed so fine and artful.
And how much more to marvel and amaze:
some birds make beds in secret hideaways
in bog or fen, on wild and wind-swept marsh,

85

on misty moorland in long mountain grass.
Her eggs lie secret, safe from the starving eye
of fox or hawk, when she takes to the sky.
Some birds build in tall trees. Some pair
in flight, conceive their young in the air.

Some quicken with their beaks, exchanging spittle,
breathing each other's breath. Some tread the female
as the peacock treads the hen to kindle her.
Who taught them how to build a house on air,
or choose the safety of the secret ground?

Observing the earth, ocean and sky I found
how I should live. Forest and field flowers
stitch the grasses with so many colours,
sour or sweet, deadly or rich with honey,
too many to name. But what has most moved me
is how the lives of beasts are purposeful
and only man, rich or poor, is most unreasonable.